★ ★ ★
OAKLAND
A's

JAMES R. ROTHAUS

CREATIVE EDUCATION

Library of Congress Cataloging-in-Publication Data

Rothaus, James.
 Oakland A's / James R. Rothaus.
  p. cm.
 ISBN 0-88682-145-2

  1. Oakland Athletics (Baseball team)   I. Title.
GV875.O24R68   1987
796.357'64'09794 — dc19

★★★
CONTENTS

Connie Mack's 50-year Reign Begins 8
Turn Of The Century Stars 12
Four Consecutive World Series (1910-13) 15
The Baseball Wars Spell Trouble For The Twenties . . 21
Three Straight Pennants! (1929-31) 21
The Moves From Philly, To Kansas City, To Oakland . 24
The Charles Finley Era (1960-1980) 25
World Champs Three Straight Years (1972-1974) . . 30
New Owners Introduce "Billy Ball" in 1980 34
Oakland Plays "Musical Managers" 37
LaRussa Heals The A's 42
LaRussa Predicts World Series 45

COVER PHOTO
Dwayne Murphy taking his customary practice cuts. (1983)

PHOTO SPREAD (PAGE 2/3)
Dwayne Murphy stretches a double into a triple by sliding safely under the glove of Boston's Wade Boggs.

Philadelphia, PA., and Oakland, CA., are about as different as two U.S. cities can be.
- Philadelphia was founded in 1682; Oakland was founded in 1854.
- Philadelphia has nearly two million people; Oakland has less than 400,000.
- Philadelphia covers 130 square miles of Pennsylvania; Oakland takes up just 54 square miles in California.
- Philadelphia is the biggest freshwater port in the world; Oakland specializes in railroad transportation.
- Philadelphia was one of the centers of the American Revolution two hundred years ago; Oakland boomed after the gold rush 100 years ago.

Though the two cities are separated by 2,800 miles of American soil, there is one very important connection between them — an exciting baseball team nicknamed the "Athletics."

The team's roots are in Philadelphia, where it began in 1901. It remained in the City of Brotherly Love for 55 years. It moved to Kansas City, Missouri, for a forgettable 13-year stay. And it settled in Oakland in 1968, where it can be found today.

During those 90-odd years, the Athletics, or A's, have made their own special mark in baseball history, including several World Series Championships, more than a dozen A.L. pennants, and an ever-growing group of legendary Hall-of-Famers.

But that's just part of the story. The team has also had two of the most colorful owners in the history of the sport — Connie Mack and Charlie Finley. It's also been managed by such famous men as Mack, Lou Boudreau, Dick Williams and Billy Martin.

1901
The Philadelphia Athletics (the team that will someday become the Oakland Athletics) plays its very first season in the new American League under legendary manager Connie Mack. Connie will manage the club for the next half-century!

PHOTO
The legendary Ty Cobb was signed by Connie Mack in the mid-1920's. Cobb brought balance and poise to the young team.

**1901
The legendary Nap Lajoie hits .422 and wins the A.L. Triple Crown.**

Some of the greatest players have worn its uniforms, including Ty Cobb, Jimmie Foxx, Lefty Grove, Satchel Paige, Tris Speaker, Rube Waddell, Vida Blue, Rollie Fingers, Catfish Hunter and Reggie Jackson.

But the early fate of the team was actually determined on December 22, 1862. That's when a boy named Cornelius McGillicuddy was born in East Brookfield, Massachusetts.

Connie Mack's 50-Year Reign Begins

No one's really sure how his name got shortened to Connie Mack. Some say childhood friends started it, others say Cornelius himself shortened it so sportswriters could fit his entire name in a baseball box score.

Mack began his baseball career as a catcher, and he became a pretty good one. At that time, pitchers were just beginning to switch from underhand to overhand tosses. Most catchers still positioned themselves as much as 15 feet behind home plate. Connie Mack was one of the first catchers to move into a crouch just behind the batter.

He perfected the art of chatting to the batters, to keep them from concentrating on the pitches. He was even known to "accidentally" tip their bats to disturb their swings.

But throughout his playing days, Mack was always a gentleman. When he got involved in coaching and managing, he brought that quality to the game.

His big break came one fateful day in 1901, when he bought 25 percent of the Philadelphia Athletics of the new American League. Little did the A's fans realize that Mack would manage that same team for the next 50

**PHOTO
In 1930 Jimmy Foxx held the hottest bat in the league, and led the Philadelphia Athletics into another World Series Championship.**

years.

There couldn't have been a better time for a man like Mack to embrace major league baseball. The sport didn't really have much respect at the turn of the century. In fact, many people viewed baseball games as just a small step above the cheap little carnivals that were so popular then.

But Connie Mack brought a dignity to the game that would soon make it the country's national sport.

How did he do it? By simply being himself. At 6-foot-1, 150 pounds, Mack knew he didn't look good in those baggy uniforms all the players were wearing. He dressed in a dark suit, with a high collar and tie, and always completed his outfit with a straw hat or derby.

He *looked* like he was serious about his sport, and he acted the part, too. He called his players by their given names. Chief Bender, for example, was never "Chief," but "Albert." The players, in turn, always called the team's owner and manager, "Mr. Mack."

Mack never swore, he never argued with an umpire, and he was never thrown out of a game in 50 years of managing.

Dignity alone, of course, wasn't enough to make the A's winners. Mack was an excellent judge of talent, a specialist at dealing with his players, and his knowledge of the game earned him the nickname, "The Tall Tactician."

Today he is considered one of baseball's true heroes, but Connie Mack wasn't perfect. He may not have had many faults, but he did have one big one. He was very tight with his money. That characteristic was to prove costly to the A's in future years. But in 1901, when the team was just getting off the ground, Mack wasted no

**1902
The A's win their first A.L. pennant. Sluggers Danny Murphy, Lave Cross, Osee Schreckengost, Socks Sevbold, Harry Davis and Dave Fultz all have .300-plus seasons.**

**PHOTO
Tris Speaker's bat was strong, but his fielding was even stronger. For a decade Speaker ruled in center field.**

1905
The A's win the A.L. pennant, earning the right to play in major league baseball's very first World Series.

PHOTO
Facing Satchel Paige's evil eye was never an easy task for enemy batters. Here, Satch pitches for the minor-league Marlins before starring for the A's.

time in putting together the team he wanted.

Turn-Of-The-Century Stars

Right from the start, Mack sought out the best talent he could find — and afford. In 1901, when the A's placed fourth in the American League, Mack already had two future Hall-of-Famers on his roster — Nap Lajoie and Eddie Plank.

Napoleon Lajoie had been playing for the National League's team in Philadelphia. Mack contacted him and offered to more than double his salary — from the N.L.'s limit of $2,400 a year, to $6,000 — *if* Lajoie would join the A's. Nap couldn't pass up that offer, and the power-hitting second baseman traded uniforms.

The move paid off. That very first A. L. season, Lajoie not only reached the magical batting average of .400, he demolished it, hitting .422. He won the A.L. Triple Crown by leading in home runs (14), and RBIs (125).

He played just four seasons (1901, 1902, 1915, 1916) with the A's. But his performances during those years helped him finish his career with some amazing statistics. He hit more than .350 seven times, with a career average of .339. He stroked 3,251 hits, including 657 doubles, and he won four league batting titles.

While Lajoie was dominating A's opponents at the plate, Eddie Plank was strutting his stuff from the pitcher's mound. Mack signed Plank right out of Gettysburg College. Although Eddie was nearly 26 years old that first season, he won 17 games for Philadelphia. In 1902, he got a 20-win season, the first of eight in his career. Plank pitched for the A's until 1914. When he retired, he had won 327 games, the first left-handed

1910
Pitcher John Coombs wins 31 games, including 13 shutouts, to lead the A's to the A.L. pennant. He then wins three games in six days in the World Series to make the A's World Champs.

PHOTO
Jack Coombs was a terror on the mound in the 1910 Series.

pitcher to win 300 in the American League.

In 1902, the A's had six .300-hitting regulars — Danny Murphy, .313; Lave Cross, .339; Ossee Schreckengost, .324; Socks Sevbold, .317; Harry Davis, .303; and Dave Fultz, .302.

In 1902, Mack added another southpaw, George Edward Waddell, to his pitching staff. That move proved to be very valuable to the future of the team.

Waddell, whom Mack called "George," of course, and everyone else called "Rube," came to Philadelphia from the N.L.'s Pittsburgh club in mid-season. Still, he won 24 games that season and led with 210 strikeouts.

The Rube was an unusual character. Years later, Mack would say without hesitation that Waddell had the best combination of speed, curve and control of any pitcher Mack had seen. But Waddell never did really grow up. He had a short attention span, and he was known to forget about baseball at times to pursue more interesting activities. Like the time he was scheduled to pitch, but left the field instead to ride in a fire engine. Or when he left in mid-season to go fishing . . . or play with marbles . . . or act as a drum major in a town band . . . or wrestle with alligators . . . or well, you get the idea. But Mack, remember, could work with almost any player, and got more out of Waddell than any other manager.

With Waddell's help, the A's won 83 games and lost 53 to win the A. L. pennant in 1902. But at that time, there was no World Series reward; the rival National League would not formally agree to hold that championship series until 1905. So Mack just kept building his team, which finished second in 1903 (with the addition of Charles Albert "Chief" Bender) and fifth in 1904,

1911
Frank "Home Run" Baker stars, as the A's take their second straight World Championship.

before winning the pennant again in 1905. That earned the A's the distinction of being in the first World Series.

That 1905 World Series didn't quite turn out as Mack wanted. The A's came face-to-face with one of the best pitchers ever—Christy Mathewson of the New York Giants. Going into the Series, many fans were looking forward to the match-up between Mathewson and Waddell, but it was not to be. The Rube injured his left shoulder in a playful scuffle with teammate Andy Coakley before the Series even began. Waddell didn't throw a pitch for the A's until the next year.

Mathewson won three games, all shutouts, and held Philadelphia to 14 hits in those three games. Ironman Joe McGinnity also delivered a shutout to the A's sluggers. Despite Chief Bender's 3-0 win, the Giants beat Philadelphia, 4 games to 1.

It was back to the drawing board for Mack. He and his team took five more years before they would win another A. L. pennant and go to the World Series.

Four Consecutive World Series (1910-13)

When the 1910 season began, the A's were up to something special. They would string together four seasons that would rank them among the best of baseball's championship dynasties.

From 1910-13, the A's had a few more future Hall-of-Famers added to their roster, including Eddie Collins and Frank Baker, who anchored Philadelphia's famous $100,000 infield; righthanded pitcher Stan Coveleskie; and southpaw Herb Pennock. Help came from pitcher Jack Coombs and fielders Amos Strunk, Rube Oldring, Dan Murphy and Socks Seybold.

Philadelphia wasted no time in 1910. The A's won 102 games and moved on to the World Series. There they downed the N. L. Champion Chicago Cubs in five games, behind star performances by two players — Collins and Baker.

Collins had taken over for Nap Lajoie at second base for the A's, and he filled those shoes well. He was faster than Lajoie, although he didn't hit with as much power or grace. He was a patient, left-handed batter who had a career average of .333. Collins led the A. L. in stolen bases four times, and had 10 alone in 1910. His career stolen-base mark of 743 is second in A. L. history, and third in the major leagues.

In the 1910 Series, Collins hit .429 and stole 4 bases. Frank Baker hit .409. And when an injury to Dedie Plank's arm knocked him out of the fall classic, Jack Coombs assumed pitching responsibilities — and won three games in six days. As a team, the A's batted .316 in the Series, which stood as an A.L. record until 1960.

The 1911 Series looked like a replay of the 1905 match-up between the A's and the New York Giants. Christy Mathewson was still firing fastballs for the Giants. He was in the midst of a 14-year string during which he would win 20 or more games 13 times, and 30 or more four times. But in 1911, even Mathewson couldn't prevent errors by his teammates. Those errors, plus another legendary performance by Frank Baker, gave the A's the World Championship, 4 games to 2.

By the way, during the 1911 World Series, Frank Baker hit two home runs in two days. Now, that might not sound like a big deal. But baseball in those days was played with a strange type of ball — a soft, tobacco-stained sphere that would hardly travel across the street

1913
Eddie Collins and Frank Baker sizzle in the World Series against the Giants. The A's win their third World Championship in four years.

1916
After losing several key players to the upstart Federal League, the A's find themselves in the American League cellar where they will stay for nearly a decade.

in a neighborhood game today. Baker blasted that dead old ball out of the park nine times total that season, to lead the American League. But it wasn't until those two World Series round-trippers had dropped in the stands that Baker received the nickname he's still known by today—"Home Run" Baker.

No one expected less than a third straight world title from Philadelphia in 1912. As Connie Mack himself said, "They had everything that year—skill, experience and confidence that comes with winning."

Mack believed that no baseball team could be called a true champion unless it had won three straight league titles, and hopes were high that 1912 would prove the A's to be such champions.

"But," Mack said, as he explained how Philadelphia let the Boston Red Sox beat them for the A. L. pennant that season, "some of them got hurt, some of them were overconfident and some broke training. So they lost the pennant. But they learned their lesson that year and came back strong in 1913 and 1914."

Strong, indeed. In 1913, the A's looked as if they were reliving the 1911 season. Home Run Baker averaged .454 in the five-game Series against the Giants; Eddie Collins batted .421 and stole three bases. Philadelphia won its third World Series in four years by a 4-1 margin in championship games.

The A's continued to get stronger in the 1914 regular season. They had won 90 games in 1912 . . . 96 in 1913 . . . and now 99 games, the club's third-best total ever. When the fall classic began, however, Philadelphia was stopped from taking its fourth crown by a group known in baseball history books as "The Miracle Braves" from Boston. The upstart Braves had surged from last place

PHOTO
Hall-of-Famer Eddie Collins was part of Philadelphia's famous $100,000 infield in 1912.

18

on July 4 to win the N. L. pennant. They swept the first four games from Mack's charges. The Series loss itself was only the beginning, however. The Philadelphia dynasty was about to end.

The Baseball Wars Spell Trouble For The Twenties

The trouble began when a new rival baseball league formed in 1913. It was called the Federal League, and its aim was much like that of the American League when it was born at the turn of the century. Unlike the A. L., the Federal League itself did not last. But the problems it caused did persist in Philadelphia for years to come.

The Federal League, like the A. L. in 1901, offered much higher salaries to any A. L. or N. L. players who would leave their teams and join the new league. Few did, but among those who joined "The Feds" in 1915 were Chief Bender and Eddie Plank. Most A. L. and N.L. owners kept their stars at home by simply raising their salaries enough to keep them happy.

That's where Connie Mack's stinginess began to hurt the A's. He refused to pay what he thought were extravagant salaries to his ball players. As a result, the quality of the Philadelphia teams dropped—quickly. The next year they found themselves in the American League cellar. They stayed in eighth place for seven seasons, and didn't really begin to recover until 1925.

Three Straight Pennants! (1929-31)

Alert Baseball fans noticed Philadelphia's gradual climb back into contention. In 1925, the A's were sec-

1925
William Lamar goes on a 29-game hitting streak, an all-time club high.

PHOTO
In 1902, Eddie Plank hurled a 20-win season, the first of eight in his career.

1929
The A's win the World Series, thanks to miraculous pitching from Howard Ehmke who throws 13 strikeouts in the opener against the Chicago Cubs.

ond in the A.L.; in 1926, they placed third; in 1927 and 1928, they recorded two more seconds. All Mack's planning finally fell into place in 1929.

The A's won 104 games that season. Al Simmons, Jimmie Foxx, Mickey Cochrane and Bing Miller carried the big bats; Joe Boley and Max Bishop teamed up for defensive plays at second base; and starting pitchers Lefty Grove, George Earnshaw and George "Rube" Walberg mowed down A.L. lineups, with relief help from Eddie Rommell and Jack Quinn.

Mack knew long before the end of the season that the A's would win the pennant. Over in the N.L., the Chicago Cubs, too, were overwhelming their opponents, and were also obvious pennant winners.

One day, about a month before the 1929 regular season ended, Connie Mack called Howard Ehmke, a 35-year-old veteran pitcher, into his office. Ehmke knew that Mack was going to release him, but Ehmke believed he had one good game left in his aging arm, and he told Mack that. "I think you're right," Mack said, and he began to hatch a scheme. "Take the next month off," Mack told Ehmke, "and follow the Cubs around for their last games. Study their batters, learn their strengths and weaknesses, and I'll start you in the first game of the World Series. But don't tell a soul."

Ehmke did as he was told, and when the first Series game was about to begin, Mack waited until the final moment before picking a starting pitcher—Ehmke.

Even Mack's own players couldn't believe it, and the Cubs were dumbfounded. With great pitchers like Grove, Earnshaw and Walberg, Mack was starting this old guy against the awesome power of Chicago's Rogers Hornsby, Kiki Cuyler, Hack Wilson and Riggs Stephen-

PHOTO
In 1942 Charles "Chief" Bender looked back with fond memories to the days when he was an ace pitcher for the powerful Athletics.

1930
The A's repeat as World Champs, downing St. Louis in the Series.

son. Yes sir, and with Mack's reputation, it's easy to guess what happened.

Ehmke was a slowball pitcher, and his molasses pitches came floating toward the plate so slowly that the Cubs sluggers couldn't get a good piece of the ball. One would go out swinging . . . another would pop up . . . another would fly out . . . and another would just stand in frustration and be called out on strikes.

When the game was over, the A's had won, 3-1, and Ehmke, the aging slow-baller, had set a Series record of 13 strikeouts. Years later, Mack would admit that Ehmke's win in the 1929 World Series was his biggest thrill in baseball.

Mack had the Cubs beat after that first, befuddling game. Philadelphia won the '29 Series in five contests, and went on in 1930 to beat St. Louis, 4 games to 2, for the 1930 World Championship. The A's got that all-important third straight pennant in 1931, but couldn't beat the Cardinals in the series. A centerfielder named Pepper Martin hit and stole his way to the Most Valuable Player award while leading St. Louis to the title.

The Moves From Philly, To Kansas City, To Oakland

Those glory years for the A's — 1929-1931 — occurred during some of the hardest times for the United States, marked by the stock market crash of 1929 and the Great Depression that followed. Just as the country was beginning to break out of those doldrums, however, the A's fell into hard times of their own.

The A's crash wasn't nearly as fast as their drop had been in 1915, but it lasted much longer, and was spread among three cities. In 1932, Philadelphia finished second in the American league; in 1933, third; in 1934, fifth. Then, in 1935, the A's hit bottom, eighth place. For the next 34 years, from 1935 through 1967, they finished eighth 13 times, and seventh 6 times. When the A.L. expanded to 10 teams in 1961, the A's were tenth 3 times, and ninth twice. During those 34 years, the highest finish the once-proud team could manage was fourth.

The team still had some good players, but no new Hall-of-Famers, except for legendary pitcher Satchel Paige, who played for the A's for just one season, 1965.

Connie Mack finally retired after the 1950 season; he was 73-years-old.

In 1955, citing lack of interest by Philadelphia fans, A's management moved the club to Kansas City. But the A's never really established themselves there. In 13 seasons in Kansas City, the club finished last five times, and never placed higher than sixth.

In 1961, the club changed hands again. This time the team got an owner whose personality was . . . well, "different" from any other owner in major league history. Even today, the mere mention of his name triggers smiles, scowls or shudders as baseball fans recall the one-and-only Charles O. Finley.

1931
The A's win the A.L. pennant. Grove ties the club record by pitching for 31 victories, including a string of 16 straight.

The Charles Finley Era (1960-1980)

In December of 1960, Charlie Finley paid $1.9-million for 52 percent of the Kansas City A's. Two months later, he paid another $1.9-million for the other 48 percent. Now he owned the entire team. Although he would hire a string of different managers in the years to come, it was clear from the start that Charlie O. was in charge of the team.

1932
Jimmie Foxx belts an all-time club record 58 homers, including three grand slams, and gets a total of 438 bases for the year.

Finley was a wealthy man, and he was used to getting his own way. He was creative, stubborn and confident. He insulted his managers, coaches and players, yet still kept their respect.

Finley was always thinking about ways to improve the game of baseball and bring more fans to the park. He had many pet projects. Some, including night games for the World Series, colored uniforms and the designated hitter, were accepted by the other teams. Others, such as orange baseballs, a three-ball walk, two-strike strikeout, the designated runner, and a mechanical rabbit that delivered new baseballs to the umpire, never caught on.

To encourage fan participation with the team, Finley introduced Bat Day, Cap Day, Hot Pants Day, T-Shirt Day, Helmet Day, Sportsmans Day, Farmers Day, Auto Industry Day and Shriners Day.

Finley loved to call his managers on the dugout telephone to request a lineup change or discuss strategy. He prided himself on being a great cook. He kept close track of his money, was usually generous with bonuses, but paid practically nothing at all if a player asked for it. Charles Finley was what some people would call "a character," although many have used stronger language to describe his colorful personality.

No matter how you look at him, though, you can't deny his impact on baseball in general, and the A's in particular. For 20 years, Charlie Finley *was* the A's.

Though Finley moved the club to Oakland in 1968, he began building the club's roster while still in Kansas City. In 1962, he signed shortstop Bert Campaneris as a free agent. Two years later, pitcher Jim "Catfish" Hunter joined the team. Catcher Gene Tenace, outfielder Joe Rudi and relief pitcher Rollie Fingers came aboard in

PHOTO
Good-bye baseball! Here's Gene Tenace launching one of his three grand slams in '74.

1965. Through the major league draft, Finley signed Rick Monday and Sal Bando that same year, Reggie Jackson in 1966, and Vida Blue in 1967.

The fans in Kansas City had mixed emotions when the A's moved to Oakland. They didn't like to see the team leave town, but many were glad to see Finley go.

In their first season on the West Coast (1968) the A's finished sixth. But in 1969, they won 88 games for second place, their most wins and highest finish since 1932.

The 1969 season is best remembered as the year Reggie Jackson burst into the limelight. For much of the season, he hit home runs at a pace that matched the single-season records of Ruth (60) and Maris (61). The pressure on the young slugger was tremendous; he was the hottest draw in the league. Jackson eventually tailed off and finished the season with 47 home runs, but he had served notice to American League pitchers. They'd have to contend with Reggie Jackson for many years to come.

The A's won 89 games in 1970, despite a lengthy and disturbing salary feud between Finley and Reggie Jackson. Reggie missed much of spring training, and got off to a slow start. Finley then told manager John McNamara to "bench Jackson for a while." The big left-handed slugger never got untracked. He batted just .237 with 23 home runs and 66 RBIs. The rift between Finley and Jackson was just one of many problems.

Dick Williams became Oakland manager in 1971, and the A's sizzled with 101 wins. Williams was a tough, no-nonsense manager. Four years earlier, he had led the Boston Red Sox to their famous "Impossible Dream" season, so he knew what it took to make a winner. He was the perfect manager for the A's.

1933
Robert Johnson launches an all-time A's rookie record 21 homers.

PHOTO
Mudcat Grant teamed with Vida Blue, Campaneris, Bando and Reggie Jackson to spark the A's of the early 70s.

1950
The great Connie Mack retires after his 50th season as A's manager.

Vida Blue was Oakland's rookie sensation in 1971. Though he lost his opening game, Blue won his next 10 straight and finished the season with 24 wins, a 1.82 earned run average and 301 strikeouts.

Meanwhile, Jackson hit 32 homers, Bando blasted 24, and first baseman Mike Epstein added 19. With help from Green, Campaneris, Tonny Davis, Mudcat Grant, Rollie Fingers, Diego Segui, Dobson, Odom and Hunter, Williams led the A's to a first place finish in the new Western Division of the American League. But they couldn't overcome Baltimore in the A.L. playoffs, and the Orioles won the pennant.

World Champs Three Straight Years (1972-74)

Finley traded Rick Monday to the Cubs for pitcher Ken Holtzman in 1972. The A's finally had their team. They defeated Detroit in the playoffs to seize the club's first A.L. pennant in 40 years. Next it was Cincinnati's famous "Big Red Machine" in the '72 World Series.

Little did the Reds suspect that the player who would seal their doom in that Series would be little-known Gene Tenace, the Oakland catcher who had hit a paltry 1-for-17 in the playoffs with Detroit. For some reason, Tenace came to life in the Series, getting eight hits in 23 at-bats for a .348 average, including four home runs, one double, nine RBIs and a .913 slugging average. Tenace, of course, was named Most Valuable Player of the Series. Oakland beat Cincinnati, 3-2, in the seventh and final game to win the first of three straight World Championships.

Now, Oakland became was one of the country's best-loved teams. They were relaxed, young ball players who

PHOTO
Whiff 'em artist Vida Blue pitched an amazing 301 strikeouts in the 1971 campaign.

didn't hesitate to say what they thought. The entire team grew moustaches after Finley had a "Moustache Day" promotion, and the team was nicknamed "The Moustache Gang." They fought among themselves, like members of a family would, and they fought with Finley, both publically and privately.

Like the A's previous dynasties in 1910-14 and 1929-31, pitching was this club's strength. Catfish Hunter was the cream of the crop. Holtzman would win 77 games in four years with the A's, and Rollie Fingers would shine as the best relief pitcher in the history of the A.L.

The Oakland defense was led by Dick Green at second base, and Campaneris at shortstop.

Many believe the 1973 A's, who beat the New York Giants, 4 games to 3, in the World Series were the best of the three-year dynasty. But the Series was marred by an ugly incident caused by Finley. When infielder Mike Andrews made two errors in one of the World Series games, Finley tried to place him on the injured list and sneak a substitute player on the Oakland roster. A's players, Williams and even Bowie Kuhn, the commissioner of baseball, were outraged and forced Finley to reinstate Andrews. He did, but Dick Williams decided that he'd had enough of Finley's antics. After the World Series win, he resigned as Oakland manager.

Alvin Dark, who had managed the A's for Finley when the club was in Kansas City, was re-hired in 1974. He led Oakland to its easiest of the three titles, a 4-1 World Series win over the Los Angeles Dodgers.

If only that super Oakland team was able to stick together, it might have matched the great record of the New York Yankees — five straight pennants and four straight World Series crowns. But it was not to be. Cat-

1955
The A's move to Kansas City and finish fifth under Manager Lou Boudreau.

PHOTO
The great Jim Hunter got the nickname "Catfish" from Charlie Finley as a publicity stunt.

33

1960
The controversial Charlie Finley purchases the A's. The stars that year are pitcher Buddy Daley who wins 16 games including nine in a row, and Ray Herbert who scatters 256 hits for the season.

PHOTO
The man with the magnificent moustache—and the vicious slider. Rollie Fingers was baseball's greatest reliever of the 1970's. (1975)

fish Hunter became a free agent and signed with the Yankees the next year. Finley traded Jackson and Holtzman, neither of whom wanted to play for the A's owner. Rudi, Fingers, Bando, Tenace and Campaneris played out their options and signed with other teams. Once again, an A's dynasty was about to crumble.

New Owners Introduce "Billy Ball" In 1980

The drop-off wasn't sudden. In 1975, the A's won the Western Division, but the surprising Boston Red Sox embarrassed Oakland in three games for the pennant. The next season, the A's took second. But in 1977, 1978 and 1979, they could only manage one sixth-place finish and two sevenths.

Charlie Finley continued to hire and offend new managers. From '75-79, the A's had nine different ones.

Then, in 1980, the tide finally took another positive turn for the Athletics when Finley sold the club to a group led by Walter J. Haas, Jr., and president Roy Eisenhardt. One of the first moves by the new owners was to hire the one-and-only Billy Martin.

Martin was like Charlie Finley in some ways. He was a fiery, colorful character who created controversy both as a player and as a manager. He starred for seven clubs during his 12-year playing career, but he was best-known as a player and manager for the New York Yankees. During his first two seasons as manager of the Yanks he took the team to a pennant and a World Championship. His feuds with Yankee owner George Steinbrenner were famous.

But the Billy Martin who came to Oakland in 1980 was all business. His double job as manager and direc-

1968
Finley moves the A's to Oakland where an all-star lineup that includes Catfish Hunter, Gene Tenace, Joe Rudi, Rollie Fingers, Sal Bando, Vida Blue, Reggie Jackson and Rick Monday finishes sixth in the A.L.

tor of player development gave him the freedom to build the team he wanted — and that's the way Billy liked it.

In just one season, Martin transformed the A's from a last-place club into one of the most exciting young teams in the league. They called Oakland's brand of baseball "Billy Ball."

The power of Tony Armas and the speed of Rickey Henderson led the '80 A's. Armas hit 35 homers and drove in 109 runs; Henderson stole an A.L. record 100 bases. Oakland's outfield, with Armas, Dwayne Murphy and Henderson, was called the best in baseball.

Meanwhile, the Oakland pitchers built a reputation for starting what they finished. By season's end, they had set a new record of 94 complete games. Rick Langford alone completed 28 of 33. At one point in the season, he went 22 straight games without being relieved. That was the longest such stretch since 1904!

No question about it. Billy Ball was working wonders in Oakland, just as it had in New York. Martin was back in the spotlight as 1980 Manager of the Year — but that was just the warm-up.

From the first crack of the bat in the 1981 campaign, the A's served notice that they would play a sizzling, run-and-gun "take no prisoners" style in every game. They won their first eleven and never looked back.

"We're aggressive, that's the thing," smiled Henderson, who led the A.L. in runs, hits and steals.

"Billy told me to swing for the fence, so that's what I did," said Tony Armas, who launched 22 homers to tie for the league long-ball title.

Murphy was busy, too. He led the league in RBIs. And, of course, the ironmen were back on the mound.

Rick Langford finished 18 games; Steve McCatty, 16.

When the dust had cleared, the "Amazin' A's," (as they were now being called) had swept the Kansas City Chiefs and their superstar, George Brett, in three straight to win the Western Division.

Oakland then met the arch-rival New York Yankees in the A.L. Pennant series. Martin figured he had a grudge to settle with Yankees' owner George Steinbrenner, his old boss. But New York's power and experience proved to be too much for the young A's. Oakland fell in three.

"The Yankees beat us," Martin shrugged, "but nobody expected us to be here anyhow."

What Billy said was true. The team that had been everyone's pushover just two years earlier had magically pulled itself up to the top of the league.

A big ad was placed by the team in local newspapers, just to tie the amazin' season off in a nice little bow. The headline simply read, "Billy Ball." Written below was this message:

"Magic is the only word for it — the voices, the music, the summer nights, the season. Thanks to the greatest fans in all of baseball, for a year we'll never forget. Spring training begins February 15th and, frankly, we can hardly wait."

1969
Reggie Jackson launches an all-time Oakland A's high of 47 homers to get his first real taste of superstardom.

Oakland Plays "Musical Managers"

Poof! As quickly as it had come, the magic was gone in 1982, and so was Billy Martin.

"I don't make excuses," said Billy as he prepared to pack his bags after what turned out to be one of the most disappointing seasons of his career. In all fairness,

1971-75
The A's modern dynasty wins five consecutive division championships, three A.L. pennants and three World Championships. Dick Williams and Alvin Dark are the managers.

though, it should be pointed out that Martin really *was* the victim of some bad breaks in '82, a campaign in which the A's went from "champs to chumps" by slumping to their worst record in 14 years.

For starters, an endless string of injuries to key players reduced Oakland's run-and-gun to limp-and-gimp.

Starting catcher Mike Heath began the season on the disabled list, and then the rest of the infield and outfield fell like dominoes. Jim Spencer, Tony Armas, Cliff Johnson, Dwayne Murphy, Mickey Klutts — all went down and out with a pulled this, or a sprained that.

Then the pitchers. Steve McCatty and Jeff Jones, shoulder problems. Mike Norris, tendinitis. Rick Langford, elbow pain.

On and on it went. Even the indestructible Rickey Henderson wrenched a shoulder and was sidelined for awhile. Fortunately, the injury occurred *after* the fleet-footed super-thief had already broken Lou Brock's record for season stolen bases. As it turned out, Rickey's achievement was the only magic moment for the A's in an otherwise dreary season.

So Billy Martin stepped down as manager, and that began what one sportswriter later termed "a game of musical managers by the Oakland front office." No sooner would one manager settle down in the skipper's chair than another would come in and take it away.

In 1982, rookie manager Steve Boros inherited the A's continuing plague of injuries. Fifteen players hit the disabled list that year. Boros responded by placing as many as 10 rookies in the starting lineup at one time!

"Who *are* these guys?" wondered the Oakland fans, as they looked down the list of unfamiliar names in the program each night.

**PHOTO
Ferocious Joaquin Andujar posted 12 victories for the A's in '86.**

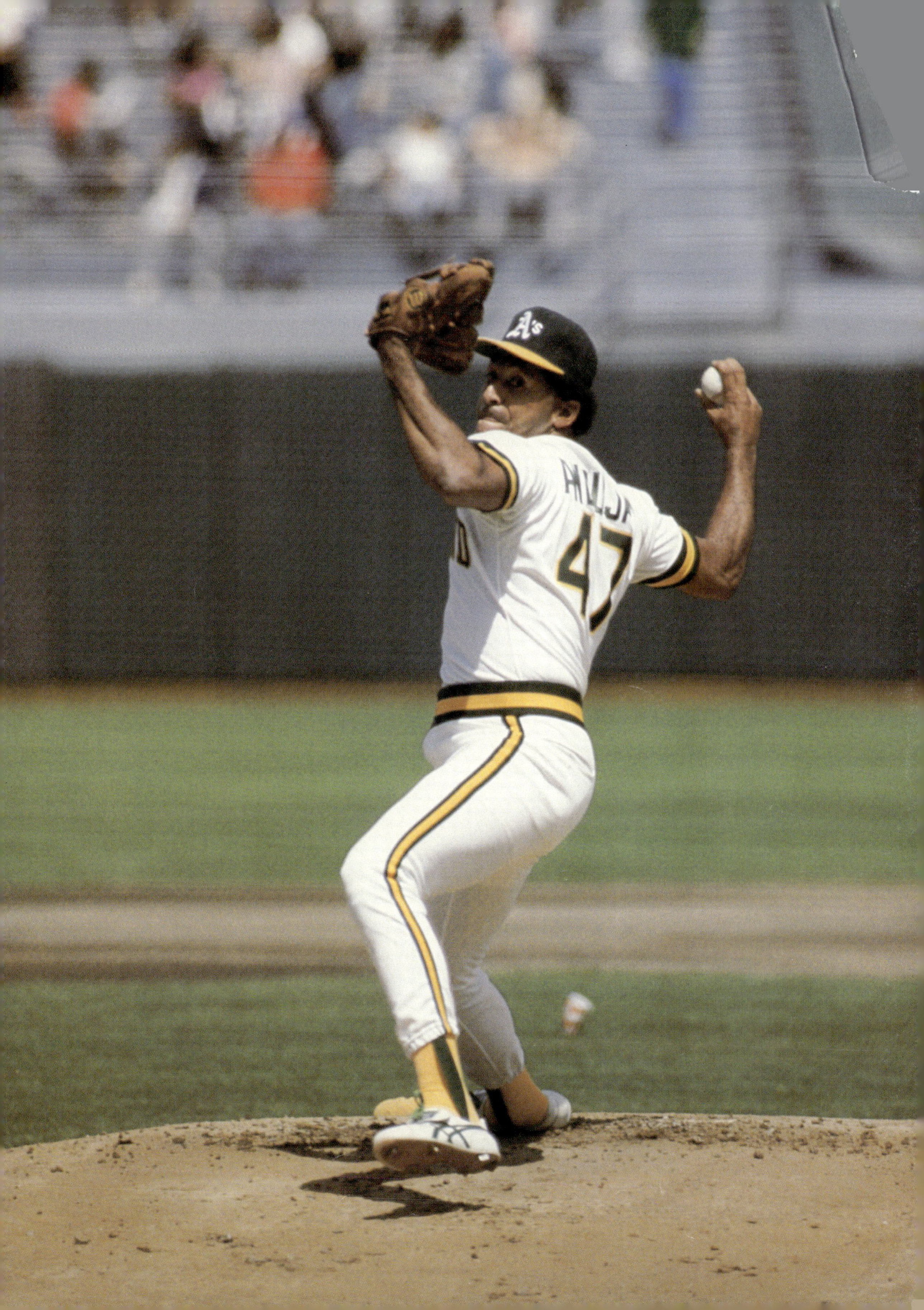

A's
47

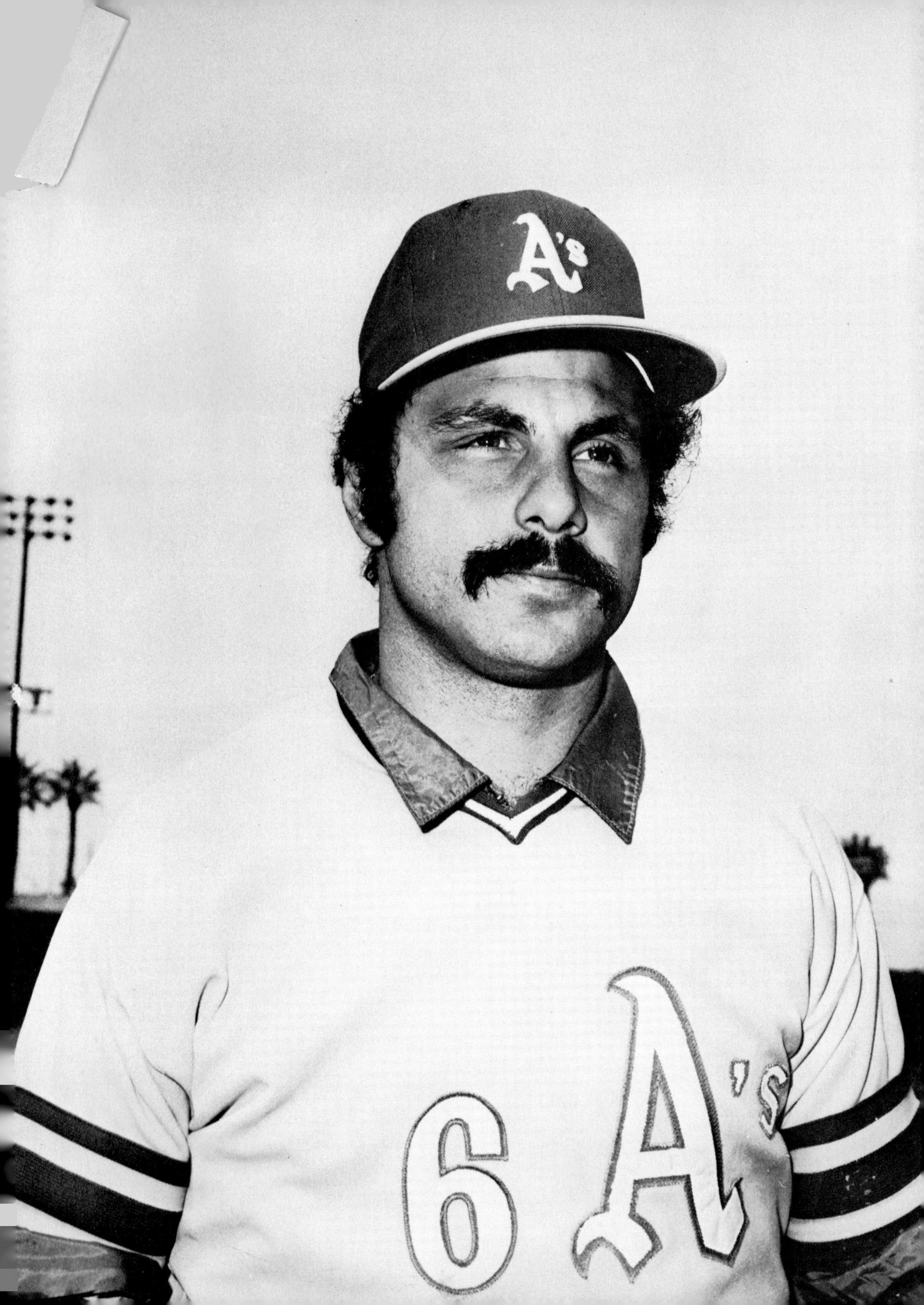
A's
6 A's

Actually, most of the first-year players did a pretty good job of filling in, and a few really sparkled. Mike Warren became the first rookie pitcher in a decade to throw a no-hitter. Right-hander Rick Codiroli, another rookie, produced 12 wins and 25 straight scoreless innings. Donnie Hill, a rookie shortstop, showed Gold Glove talent at times.

Together, the rookie manager and his rookie players were able to finish in fourth-place, one notch higher than the year before.

In 1984, some new, old faces signed on with the young A's. Dave "King Kong" Kingman, the 35-year-old home-run machine, came over from the New York Mets to help out in the power department. He was joined by little Joe Morgan, the 41-year-old superstar who had helped lead Cincinnati's "Big Red Machine" to glory in the mid-70's. Then came Bill Caudill, Bruce Bochte, Ray Burris, Jim Essian and Lary Sorenson — all gray-haired vets.

Not much help. In late May, with Oakland showing signs of a downward spiral, Boros lost his manager's chair to assistant coach Jackie Moore. Thanks to 35 homers from Kingman, key saves from Caudill, and 66 steals from Henderson, the A's were able to keep themselves out of the cellar, finishing in fourth under Moore.

In 1985, the A's were actually *two* teams. From April to August, they were the aggressive, hard-charging club that stirred up big clouds of baseline dust in ball parks from coast-to-coast.

From August to September, however, they were the team with the rubber bats and the Swiss-cheese mitts.

Ace sportswriter Kit Steir summed up the collapse in the 1986 edition of the *Official Baseball Guide:*

1980
Finley sells the A's, Billy Martin takes over as manager, and the big bats of Rickey Henderson, Tony Armas and Dwayne Murphy catapult the A's from seventh to second.

PHOTO
Sal Bando was honored as a "team leader" after Oakland defeated the New York Giants in the '73 World Series.

1984
Dave Kingman matches Reggie Jackson's record of 35 homers in a single season. Kingman will repeat the feat in '86.

"On August 10 in Seattle, the day Dave Kingman hit his 400th career home run, the A's completed a stretch in which they won 11 of 14 games to climb to their highwater mark of the season at 10 games over .500. A day later they took a 6-0 lead against the Mariners, blew it and were never heard from again. The A's won just 18 of their last 54 games to finish with a 77-85 record for the second year in a row."

Start the music. Another new skipper would soon come down the line.

LaRussa Heals The A's

The Chicago White Sox fired Tony LaRussa in June, 1986. The Oakland Athletics picked the same month to fire Jackie Moore, and then they hired — you guessed it — Tony LaRussa.

Actually, we should probably refer to the A's new skipper as "Doctor" LaRussa. No sooner had he come to town than a whole platoon of wounded A's began springing up from their sick beds to play baseball.

Ace pitcher Joaquin Andujar rebounded from a leg injury to contribute 12 victories.

Center-fielder Dwayne Murphy recovered from a back ailment in time to chip in 39 RBIs.

Jay Howell proved that his ailing arm was on the mend by returning in July to finish with 16 saves.

A healthy Dave Kingman crunched 35 homers, while third baseman Carney Lansford and right-fielder Mike Davis hit 19 apiece.

And don't forget young Jose Canseco, whose 33 homers, 117 runs and 15 pilfered bases brought him 1986 A.L. Rookie of the Year honors!

PHOTO
Major league baseball's all-time greatest base thief — Rickey Henderson — prepares to get aboard again. (1983)

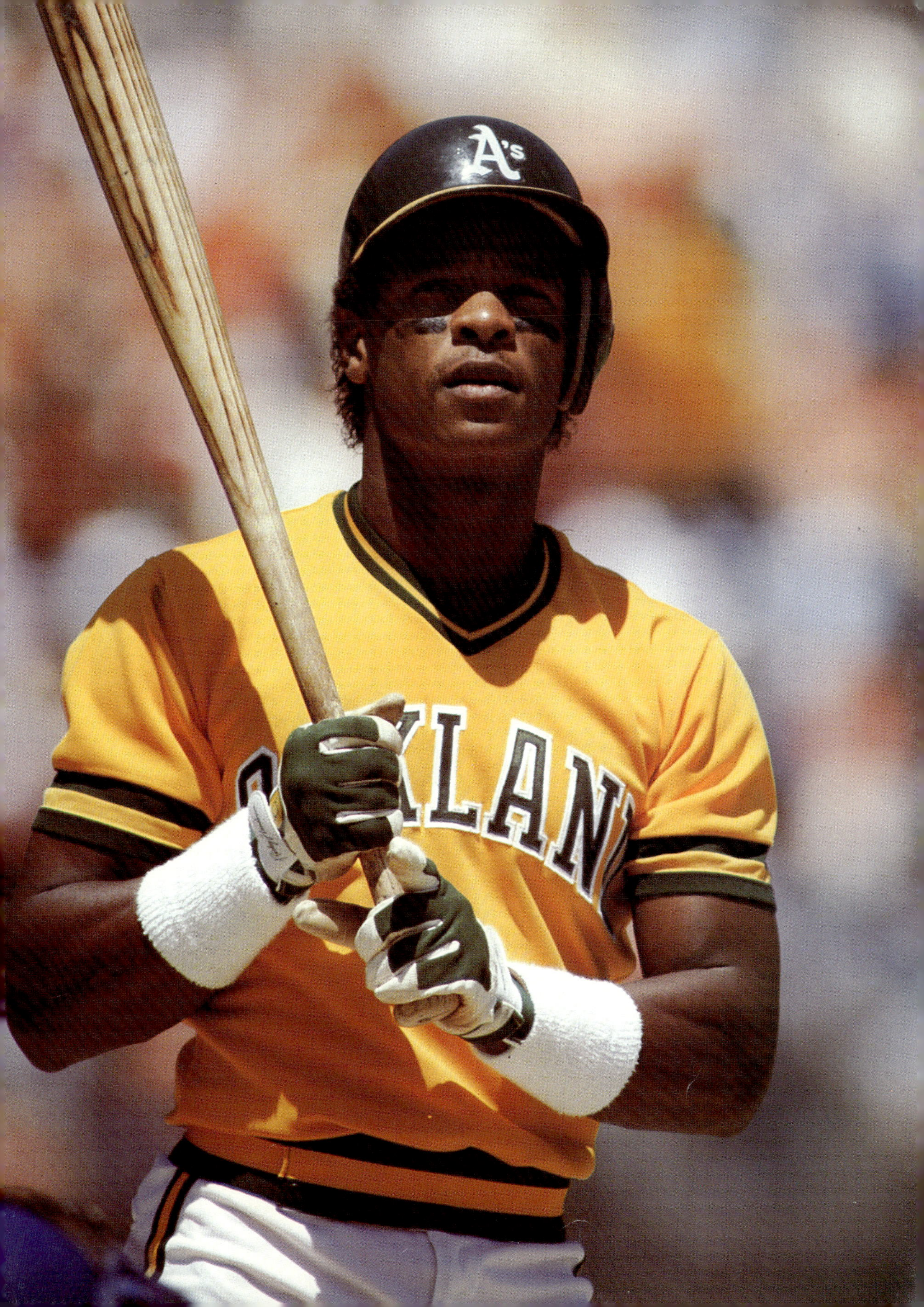
A's

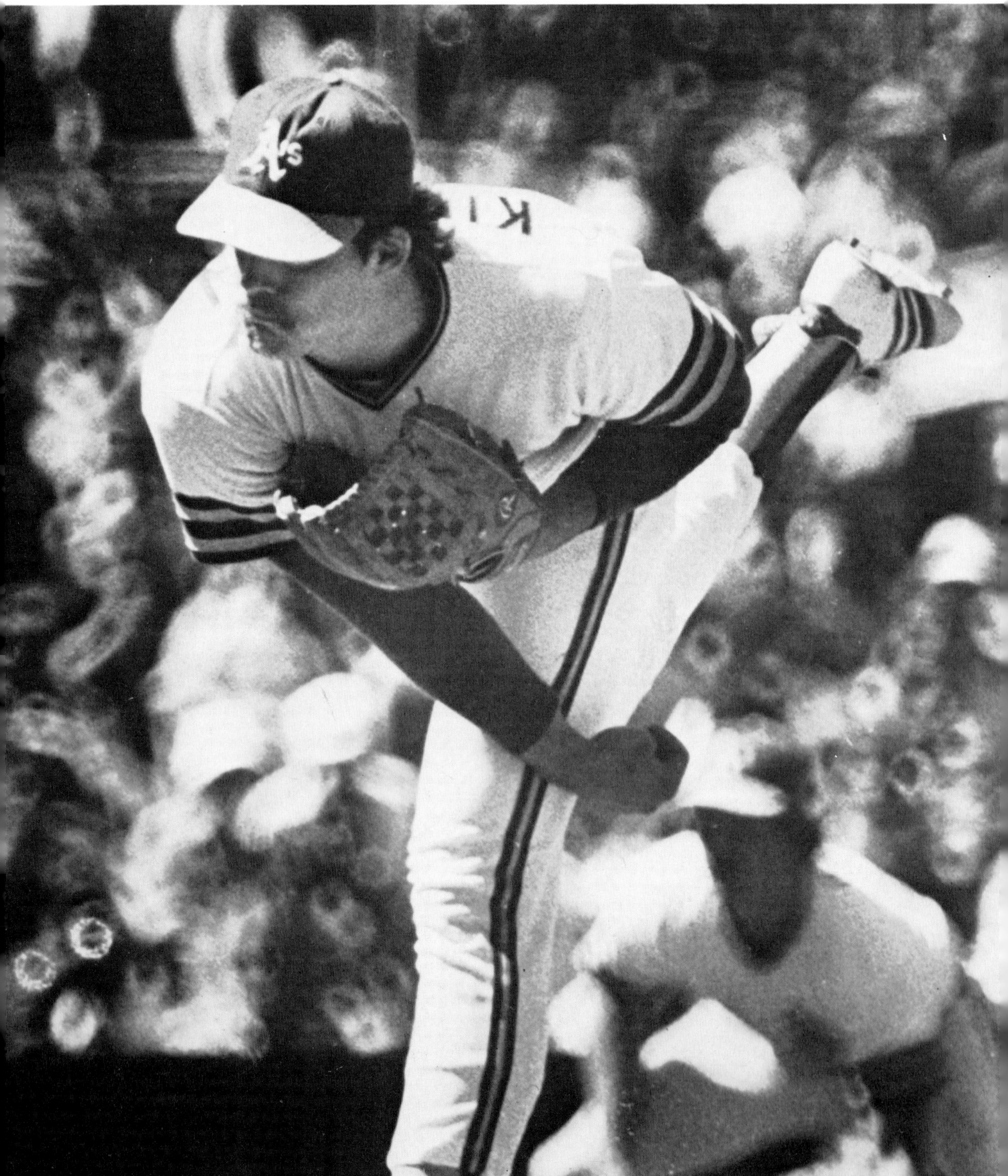

Result: The team that had started in last place under LaRussa in mid-summer regained enough ground to finish the season in a third-place tie with Kansas City. According to LaRussa, the team had regained something more important along the way—self-respect.

"You can feel it in the clubhouse," said Tony at season's end. "There's a new way of thinking around here. No fiddling around. These guys have made up their minds to play up to their ability and win some ball games."

LaRussa Predicts World Series

The good feeling carried over into 1987.

Reggie Jackson, Joe Rudi and Dave Duncan—all former players with those rollicking World Champion Oakland A's of the early 70's—were all back in Oakland uniforms.

Reggie, at 40, was wielding his big bat in DH duties. Rudi was the outfield coach, and Duncan was coaching the catchers.

Standing in the outfield were three heavy hitters in Davis, Murphy and Canseco.

The infield featured Alfredo Griffin at short, Lansford at third, Mickey Tettleton at catcher, and two mammoth rookies—6-foot-4 Rob Nelson at first, and 6-foot-5 Mark McGwire backing up Lansford at third.

The pitching roster was a familiar one—Andujar, Young, Stewart, Codiroli, Ontiveros and Howell.

"You will see aggression in our pitchers this year," promised Andujar, a fierce competitor who remained one of only two hurlers since the 1940's who had hit a grand slam homer, but never allowed one.

1987
Slugger Reggie Jackson, 40, returns to the A's to close out his career with the team that brought him his first World Championship.

PHOTO
Brian Kingman, one of the core of exciting young players who played "Billy Ball."

1987
In his first full season as Oakland Manager, Tony LaRussa predicts a World Series for the A's in "five years or less."

In late April of the '87 season, with the A's still holding their own in the middle of the standings, Tony LaRussa took time for a pre-game interview during a three-game home stand against the Seattle Mariners.

"What do you honestly think of your club?" asked the interviewer.

"I think their statistics look bad, but their performance looks good," said LaRussa, and then he paused. "The most honest thing I can say is that I believe this team will be in the World Series within five years or less."

Those great fans in Oakland, California are betting on "less."

PHOTO
Reggie Jackson helped sparked the A's to two World Championships and returned in 1987 to close out his career in Oakland green.

SOUTHWEST LIBRARY
PRATT, KANSAS